FREE VERSE POEMS

ried my father in my
Now he grows me, my strange son,
My little root who won't drink milk;
Little pale foot s in unheard-of night,
Little cloc ing newly wet
In the fire; little arent to the future
Wine, a son of his own son,
Little fathe life.

JoAnn Early Macken

Author
JoAnn Early Macken

Publishing plan research and development
Reagan Miller

Project coordinator
Kelly Spence

Editor
Anastasia Suen

Proofreader and indexer
Wendy Scavuzzo

Design
Margaret Amy Salter

Photo research
Margaret Amy Salter

Prepress technician
Margaret Amy Salter

Print and production coordinator
Margaret Amy Salter

Photographs and illustrations
All images by Shutterstock

JoAnn Early Macken is the author of *Write a Poem Step by Step* (Earlybird Press), five picture books, and 125 nonfiction books for young readers. Her poems appear in several children's magazines and anthologies. JoAnn has taught writing at four Wisconsin colleges. She speaks about poetry and writing to students, teachers, and adult writers at schools, libraries, and conferences. You can visit her website at www.joannmacken.com.

Library and Archives Canada Cataloguing in Publication

Macken, JoAnn Early, 1953-, author
        Read, recite, and write free verse poems / JoAnn Early
Macken.

(Poet's workshop)
Includes index.
Issued in print and electronic formats.
ISBN 978-0-7787-0408-9 (bound).--ISBN 978-0-7787-0412-6 (pbk.).--
ISBN 978-1-4271-7520-5 (html).--ISBN 978-1-4271-7524-3 (pdf)

        1. Free verse--Authorship--Juvenile literature. I. Title.

PN1059.F7M35 2014   j808.1   C2014-900930-5
                                                        C2014-900931-3

Library of Congress Cataloging-in-Publication Data

CIP available at Library of Congress

Crabtree Publishing Company

Printed in Canada/032014/BF20140212

www.crabtreebooks.com 1-800-387-7650

Published in Canada
Crabtree Publishing
616 Welland Ave.
St. Catharines, Ontario
L2M 5V6

Published in the United States
Crabtree Publishing
PMB 59051
350 Fifth Avenue, 59th Floor
New York, New York 10118

Published in the United Kingdom
Crabtree Publishing
Maritime House
Basin Road North, Hove
BN41 1WR

Published in Australia
Crabtree Publishing
3 Charles Street
Coburg North
VIC 3058

Contents

Chapter 1: What Is a Free Verse Poem?

The word **verse** is another word for a poem. So what is free verse? It is a poem that doesn't follow the "old" rules. Much of the way free verse is explained has to do with what it is not.

In most poems, the lines of the poem are the same length. But you don't have to do that in a free verse poem. You can make some lines short and other lines long.

In many poems, the words at the end of the lines **rhyme**. They end with the same sounds. Free verse doesn't use regular end rhyme. The words at the end of the lines don't have to rhyme with each other.

In a free verse poem, you might see rhyme in the middle of a line. The words in the middle of a line may have the same sounds. Rhyme within a line is called **internal rhyme**.

Every poem has a **rhythm**. The rhythm of a poem is how you say the words. Some syllables are **stressed** and some are not. Many poems have a steady rhythm. A free verse poem might not.

When you write free verse, you can create your own rhythm and form.

Prose vs. Drama vs. Poetry

In literature, we use different names to talk about the way words are used. As you can see in the examples below, the same story can be told in many different ways.

Prose

Once upon a time there was a daydreamer. He was sitting under an apple tree. It was the spring and the apple tree was blooming. A soft wind blew. Apple blossom petals fluttered in the wind as they fell to the ground. But the daydreamer didn't notice. His mind was in a country far, far away.

Drama

TIME: a spring morning
PLACE: under an apple tree
[The DAYDREAMER is sitting under the apple tree with his eyes closed.]
WIND: Woooo
TREE: Rustle
FLOWER PETALS: Flutter
[The wind blows and flower petals fall to the ground.]
[The DAYDREAMER doesn't move.]

Poetry

Thoughts
My thoughts keep going far away
Into another country under a different sky:
My thoughts are sea-foam and sand;
They are apple-petals fluttering.

—Hilda Conkling

We use sentences to tell a story in **prose**. When a story is performed as a play, it is called a **drama**. Can you see the stage directions? They let the actors know when and where things happen.

The third example is a **poem**. A poem uses short **phrases**, or groups of words, to tell a story or share a feeling.

5

Writing Your Own Free Verse Poem

When you write free verse, you can express what you want to say in your own voice. Read as much free verse as you can to see how other poets create their poems.

In "Thoughts," each line begins with a capital letter. Doing so was a common practice long ago when the poem was written. Many modern poets choose to capitalize only words that start new sentences. When you write, you can decide which words to capitalize.

You can also decide how and even whether to use punctuation. A **line break**, or ending, can create a pause and take the place of a comma or period.

When you write a free verse poem, you do not have to write in full sentences. In fact, using fragments or phrases might make your poem stronger.

As you write, play around with the placement of lines. Try indenting a line from the left margin for extra emphasis.

Keep your readers in mind. Use the most logical form to make your poem easier to understand.

Five Steps to Writing

1. Pre-writing: Brainstorm new ideas. Write every one down, even if it seems as though it might not work.

2. Drafting: Your first copy can be sloppy. You can always fix it later.

3. Revising: Use input from other writers to make your poem better.

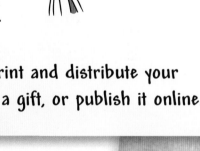

4. Editing: Check for spelling, grammar, and punctuation.

5. Publishing: Print and distribute your poem, give it as a gift, or publish it online.

About This Book

In this book, you'll learn about one type of poem: the free verse poem.

Literature Links explore the tools that all types of literature use.

Poetry Pointers explain the parts that are special to poetry.

Thinking Aloud sections include discussion questions, brainstorming tips, graphic organizers, and examples of students' writing.

Now It's Your Turn! gives you tips on how to write your very own free verse poems.

Chapter 2: Writing a Free Verse Animal Poem

Are you ready to read, recite, and write free verse animal poems? You can use your imagination. One good way to come up with an idea is to daydream. Ask yourself, "What if . . . ?" In this poem, the poet imagines what a mouse might do with the paper he has been writing on.

Salutations To A Mouse

If a mouse makes a nest
Of one's written words
Is there else to do but accept
The flattery?
I have deemed it wise to do so.
I have thanked him
Sufficiently
As he scurried in and out
Of the room.
He has faced the winter
With a nest of my words.
I did not suspect them
Of such worth against the cold.

—Marsden Hartley

Poetry Pointers: Line Breaks and Stanzas

In free verse poems, lines can be of any length. Poets often break, or end, lines where a reader would take a breath. Another logical plan is to end a line at the end of a phrase or thought. A line that ends with punctuation is called **end-stopped**.

You can also break the lines a different way. You can take one thought and break it into several lines. That's what the poet did in "Salutations To A Mouse." Carrying a thought from one line to the next is called **enjambment**.

One thought...

If a mouse makes a nest of one's written words is there else to do but accept the flattery?

...can be broken into four lines.

If a mouse makes a nest — enjambed
of one's written words — enjambed
is there else to do but accept — enjambed
the flattery? — end-stopped

Why break a line this way? The word or phrase at the end of a line gets the most attention. The word or phrase at the beginning gets the second most. However you decide to break a line, it should feel right to you. You can also add a space between the lines. This space will start a new **stanza**. That's what poets call their paragraphs. In a free verse poem, stanzas can include different numbers of lines. The lines can also be of different lengths. If your poem includes more than one idea, consider breaking it into stanzas.

9

Literature Link: Word Choice

When you write, make the best choice for every word.
How do you decide which words to use?

 Meaning is the most important factor. Be as specific as possible. Use a dictionary to find out what words mean.

 A **thesaurus** will give you lists of words that mean almost the same thing. For example: *yell*, *holler*, and *shout* all describe something similar.

 Words with similar meanings might sound very different. One might be a better fit with the language of your poem.

 Another word may be a better fit for the **tone**, or the feeling or emotion, of your poem.

 One word might fit the rhythm of your poem better than another with the same meaning.

Thinking Aloud

A fascinating fact can inspire an exciting poem. Tara's group wanted to write animal poems. They made a list of interesting animal facts.

 The arctic tern's annual migration is the longest of any bird.

Hippos spend most of the day in water. They graze on grass at night.

Bullfrogs earned their name because people thought they sounded like cows mooing.

Young flamingos are white. They turn pink or reddish from the food they eat.

When camels walk, they move both legs on one side at the same time.

Write Your Own Free Verse Animal Poem
Now It's Your Turn!

What animal do you want to write about? After you decide, use a KWL Chart. You can use the words on your chart to write your free verse animal poem.

What I Know	What I Want to Know	What I Learned

Start with what you know about that animal. Write it in the "What I Know" column. Then fill out the "What I Want to Know" part. Then do your research. Add what you found out to "What I Learned."

What I Know	What I Want to Know	What I Learned
Porcupines have sharp quills	Where do they live?	Porcupines spend most of their time up in the trees.

After Tara found this fact, she added words to describe it.

Tara wrote this poem.

In the Wildlife Refuge
High in a treetop,
a lumpy shape
clung to a bendy branch,
swung back and forth,
nibbled spring buds.
Porcupine!
We saw three that day.
One slept all curled up
on a limb overhead,
quilly and safe.
One waddled alongside
the narrow tree-lined road.

Chapter 3: Writing a Free Verse Sound Effects Poem

Can you hear it? In this chapter, you will read, recite, and write a free verse poem with sound effects. The words you use in a poem can help others hear what you are describing. Your words create an image for readers.

Writing with specific images is called **imagery**. When you write, try to use all your senses to create an image. Use details that include sight, sound, smell, touch, and taste.

As you read this poem, listen for sound effects.

The Skaters

Black swallows swooping or gliding
In a flurry of entangled loops and curves;
The skaters skim over the frozen river.
And the grinding click of their skates as they impinge upon the surface,
Is like the brushing together of thin wing-tips of silver.

—John Gould Fletcher

Poetry Pointer: Onomatopoeia

Some words sound like what they mean. These sound effect words have a fancy name. They are called **onomatopoeia** (on-*uh*-mat-*uh*-PEE-*uh*).

You just read three words like this in "The Skaters." Can you find *grinding*, *click*, and *brushing*? They are examples of onomatopoeia. The words sound like their meanings.

Literature Links: Similes and Metaphors

When you write, don't just describe your subject. To create a clear image, compare it to something else. Two kinds of imagery compare one thing to another, sometimes in surprising ways.

A **simile** is a comparison that uses *like* or *as*. In "The Skaters," the poet uses *like* to compare the sound of the skates to the sound of silver wing-tips. Here are some more examples of similes:

> round as a globe
> as fast as a peregrine falcon
> shines like a star

A **metaphor** is a comparison that does not use *like* or *as*. It can be a stronger comparison than a simile because it states that something is something else. In "The Skaters," the poet says that the skaters are black swallows. Here are some more examples of metaphors:

> Last night's homework was a breeze.
> My head was spinning.
> A blanket of snow fell over the town.

Thinking Aloud

Shawn and his group brainstormed onomatopoeia. They thought of five kinds of sounds. They made a list of five examples of each.

Animal
tweet
moo
baa
meow
woof

Mechanical
beep
honk
zoom
whack
ding-dong

Musical
ring
toot
trill
echo
whistle

Actions
Knock
pop
chomp
stomp
plop

Nature
whoosh
boom
crackle
burble
crash

What can you add to this list?

14

Write Your Own Free Verse Sound Effects Poem
Now It's Your Turn!

What do you hear? Write your own free verse sound effects poem. You can use one of the students' suggestions. Or you can invent your own characters and actions. Shawn wrote about sounds he heard in a forest.

Hike

We crunch through fallen leaves
brown as bark.
Our dog trots ahead, sniffing,
a detective on the prowl.
Tap-tap-tap-tap makes us stop,
look up
at a woodpecker circling
an old dead oak
that reaches through blue
toward the sun.

Chapter 4: Writing a Free Verse Talking Poem

In this chapter, you will read, recite, and write poems that talk to someone or something. Why not? We all have something to say.

In this poem, the poet speaks to the sea. In mythology, an Oread is a nymph. This spirit of nature appears as a young woman.

Oread

Whirl up, sea—
Whirl your pointed pines.
Splash your great pines
On our rocks.
Hurl your green over us—
Cover us with your pools of fir.

—H. D. (Hilda Doolittle)

Poetry Pointer: Repetition
To **repeat** something means to do or say it more than once. Repeating a word, a phrase, or a line is an effective poetic technique. It can help make a point or reinforce a concept.

? In "Oread," lines 1 and 2 both begin with *Whirl*. Which word repeats in lines 2 and 3?

repeat
repeat
repeat

Literature Link: Point of View

A poem that talks to someone has a special name. Speaking to the subject of a poem is called **apostrophe**.

What do you need to do to write an apostrophe poem? You need to choose a **point of view**. Who will be doing the talking in your poem?

You have three choices.

Me, me, me! **Will you choose the first person point of view? The speaker uses I, me, or we in the poem. (Psst! It doesn't really have to be you! You can always pretend to be someone or something else. You can write as though you were a cat or a pencil. This is a called a** mask **poem.)**

You, you, you! **Second person point of view speaks to someone or something. Like "Dread," it uses** *you*, **either singular or plural. To write in second person, think of someone or something you would like to speak to. What could you say?**

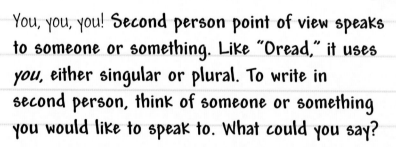

Everyone else! **A third person point of view talks about someone or something. It uses it, he, she, or they. (That's everyone except** *you* **and** *me*.**) To write in third person, think of a subject you care about. Your poem will be stronger if you write about a subject that stirs up an emotion.**

Thinking Aloud

Poetry does not have to be all about sweetness and light. Free verse can be an excellent way to express any emotion. You could give someone or something a piece of your mind. You could even reveal a secret. Your poem can be silly or serious.

Dominique's group worked together. They wrote the word "feelings" in the center and circled it. They brainstormed words about different feelings using a **cluster**. They added examples of what might cause those feelings. They circled the new words, too.

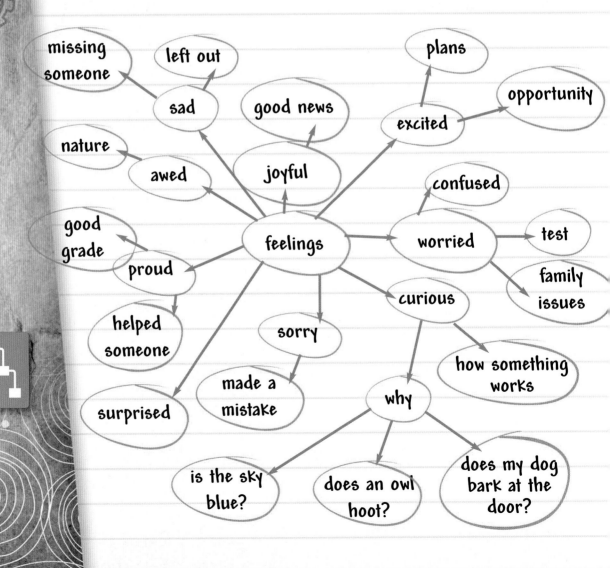

Write Your Own Free Verse Apostrophe Poem
Now It's Your Turn!

Are you ready to write your own free verse talking poem?
First you need to choose someone or something to talk to.
Then you need to decide who will do the talking. Make
your own cluster or use the same one the students used.

When you write about something you care about, put
your heart into your work. Dominique was feeling
frustrated. She wrote a poem to her heavy backpack.

Why, Backpack, Why?

Oh, backpack,
why must you be so heavy?
Why can't I fit
everything I need in you
and still pick you up?
Why can't I carry you without
bending over looking at my toes?
Why can't I find my homework
in all your bulging pockets?
Oh, backpack,
could you please be more helpful?

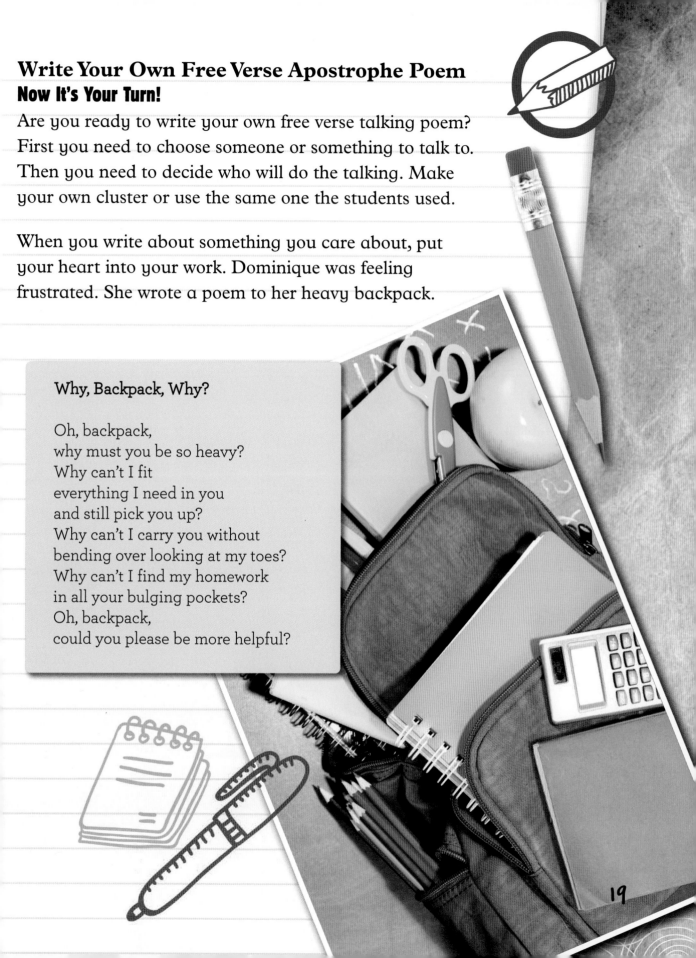

Chapter 5: Writing a Free Verse Time Poem

Time is something that we all experience. In this chapter, you will read, recite, and write free verse poems about time. In this poem, the poet writes about dusk as though it is a person.

Dusk

Dusk came over the hill to me,
Holding a red moon,
And I danced with her,
Feeling and following her starry steps,
Till she turned and gave the moon
To the swarthy night—
And slipped away without explaining.

—Witter Bynner

Literature Link: Personification

In "Dusk," the poet writes about a time of day as though it is human. Dusk holds the moon and dances.

You can do this, too. You can write about a nonliving object as though it were alive. You can also write about an animal or object as though it were a person. This is called **personification**.

Poetry Pointer: Alliteration

Poets like to repeat things. They repeat words. They repeat sounds. Can you see what repeats in this line?

Feeling and following her starry steps

Several words in a row begin with the same sound. This is called **alliteration**.

The words *Feeling* and *following* begin with the same sound. But that is not the only example. The last two words, *starry* and *steps*, also begin with the same sound.

This repetition is a pleasant pattern to hear in a poem. You can use it when you write, too!

Thinking Aloud

Luis and his group talked before they started writing. They made a time wheel. They wrote down what they did at different times of the day.

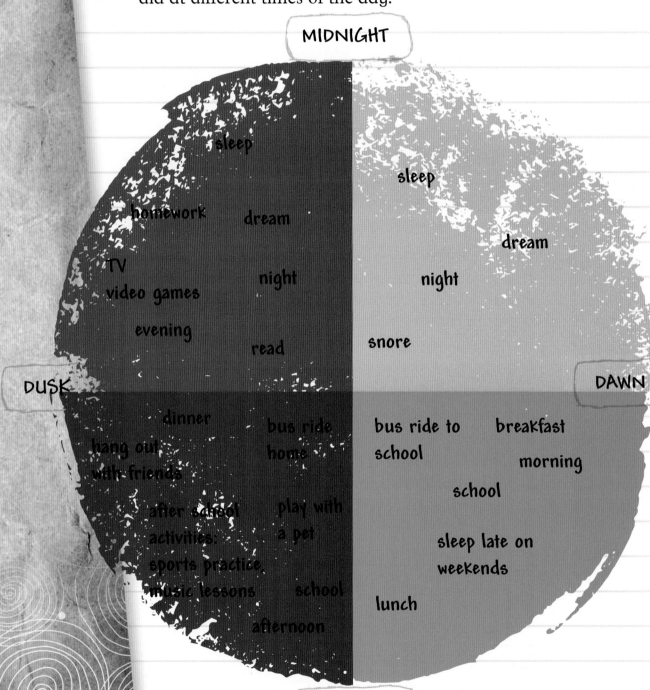

MIDNIGHT

sleep

sleep

homework

dream

dream

TV
video games

night

night

evening

read

snore

DUSK

DAWN

dinner

bus ride
home

bus ride to
school

breakfast

hang out
with friends

morning

school

after school
activities:

play with
a pet

sleep late on
weekends

sports practice,
music lessons

school

lunch

afternoon

NOON

Write Your Own Free Verse Time Poem
Now It's Your Turn!

It's time for you to write your own free verse time poem. Draw a circle and make a time wheel. Fill it up with the things that you do every day.

Then choose a time of day or night to write your poem about. In his poem, Luis imagined midnight in different ways.

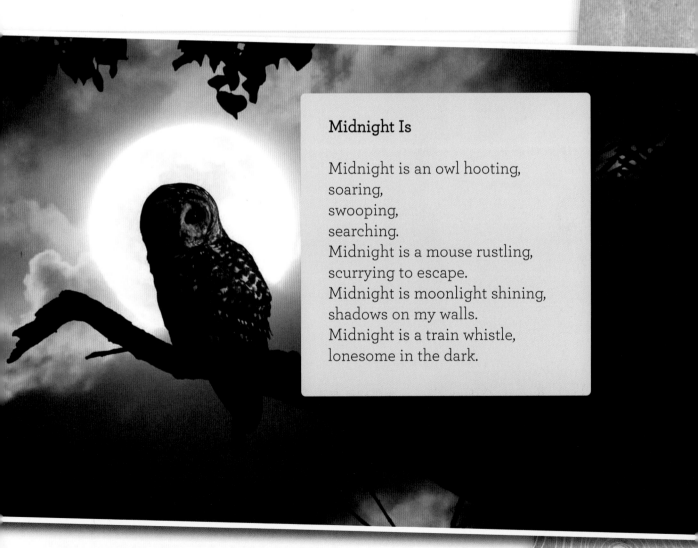

Midnight Is

Midnight is an owl hooting,
soaring,
swooping,
searching.
Midnight is a mouse rustling,
scurrying to escape.
Midnight is moonlight shining,
shadows on my walls.
Midnight is a train whistle,
lonesome in the dark.

Chapter 6: Writing a Free Verse Nature Poem

You will read, recite, and write free verse nature poems in this chapter. Poets who write about nature never seem to run out of topics. The weather inspires poem after poem.

Are all of these poems alike? No. Each poet has a unique **voice**. Each poet talks about the world in a different way. That makes their poems different.

Rain

Like crawling black monsters
the big clouds tap at my window,
their shooting liquid fingers slide
over the staring panes
and merge on the red wall.
Some of the fingers pull at the hinges
and whisper insistently: "Let us come in,
the cruel wind whips and drives us
till we are sore and in despair."
But I cannot harbor the big crawling black clouds,
I cannot save them from the angry wind.
In a tiny crevice of my aching heart
there is a big storm brewing
and loud clamour and constant prayer
for the reflection of snow-capped mountains
on a distant lake.
Tired and dazed I sit on a bear skin
and timidly listen to the concert of storms.

—William Saphier

Poetry Pointers: Consonance and Assonance

You already know that poets like to repeat sounds. But repeating the first sound in a word isn't the only way. You can also repeat sounds in the middle or the end of a word.

This repetition sounds best when it is on the same line. Can you hear the *r* sound repeating in this line?

> till we are sore and in despair."

When consonants repeat in the middle or the end of several words in a line it is called **consonance**.

If you try this with vowels, it is called **assonance**. You can see the *i* sound repeating in this line:

> and whisper insistently: "Let us come in,

Literature Link: Description

Description helps readers imagine a vivid image. On way to do this is to describe a thing. In literature, we call the word that names something, such as a person, place, or thing, a **noun**.

To describe a noun, you can add words called **adjectives**. An adjective is any word that describes a noun.

Here are some examples of adjectives and their nouns from "Rain."

Another way to add more description is to talk about the action. The word that shows action is called a **verb**. When you add more information to describe that verb, you use an **adverb**. Many adverbs end in –ly. Look for two examples in "Rain." What do they describe?

crawling black monsters

cruel wind

shooting liquid fingers

Thinking Aloud

Nature is everywhere. It offers an endless supply of inspiration. An acorn grows into an oak tree. A caterpillar crawls over a leaf. A cricket chirps.

When you write, you can describe a scene. You can explore a process. You can always discuss the weather. Here is one way to narrow your options.

1. Choose a familiar setting. Consider a place such as a mountain, forest, city, desert, or pond.

2. Think about the wildlife you might find there. Could you write about a tree or plant, an animal, a bird, or an insect?

3. Decide on the season. What happens in your setting at different times of the year? Also consider the time of day or night.

Emma and her group brainstormed ideas for their nature poems. They listed a setting and topic for each season.

season	setting	topic
spring	forest	A fawn in the shade of a tree
summer	lake	Waves wash onto the shore
fall	city	Maple leaves change color
winter	field	A hawk chases a mouse through the snow

Write Your Own Free Verse Nature Poem
Now It's Your Turn!

Nature is all around you, so write about what you know. You can choose a topic from the students' brainstorming list, or you can think up your own idea. In her poem, Emma describes a winter scene.

Snowfall

Silent snow
soft snow
flakes float
down to the ground
twirl and whirl
spin on sparkling wings
tumble and turn
gather together in gentle drifts

In the next chapter, you can see how Emma's classmates helped her revise her poem.

Chapter 7: Revising Your Free Verse Poem

Congratulations! You have just completed the first two steps of writing. You brainstormed new ideas, then you used them to write your first draft. Now you are ready for the next two steps: revising and editing. Use this checklist as a guide.

Yes/No	Revision Checklist
	1. Are your line breaks in logical places?
	2. Does the point of view match from line to line?
	3. Can you repeat something for greater effect?
	4. Did you play with words to add comparisons or sound effects?
	5. Is the description specific?

Take time to think about every comment. Then use the ones that make the most sense to you.

Group Help

One good way to revise your poem is to share it with a group. Give each person a copy. Ask them to write their comments on it. Ask one person to read your poem aloud. Listen for any places where the reader stumbles. Give the others a chance to speak before you say anything about your work.

Then move to the next writing step. Did they see anything you need to edit? Are there any spelling, grammar, or punctuation errors?

The other students thought Emma's poem created a clear picture of a wintry scene.

"The line *down to the ground* would fit better after the snow falls," said Tara.

"Maybe you can switch *gentle* and *soft*," said Shawn. "That puts *soft* and *drift* together at the end."

"I don't think you need the word *and*," said Dominique. Emma took it out of two lines.

"You can repeat the word *down*," said Luis.

"*Turn* and *spin* mean the same thing," said Emma. "I'll take one out."

Here is her revised poem.

Snowfall

Silent snow
gentle snow
flakes float
twirl
whirl
spin on sparkling wings
tumble down
down to the ground
gather together in soft drifts

Helping others revise and edit their poems can help you, too. When you read others' work, look for the positive. Point out what works well. Be supportive. Writing is not easy, and sharing can be even harder! If you don't understand something, ask a question.

Chapter 8: Performing a Poem

The final step of writing is publishing your work. After you finish the final copy of your poem, you can share it with others. You can read your free verse poem aloud to a group. You can perform your own poem!

Did you know that we have an entire month just for poems? April is National Poetry Month. It's been that way since 1996! The Academy of American Poets started it. People read and recite poetry all month long. You can do it, too!

One day in April is extra special. It's called Poem in Your Pocket Day. You do just what the name says. You put a poem in your pocket. During the day you read it aloud. You share it with others. Why not share one of your own poems?

Learning More

Books

Dark Emperor and Other Poems of the Night by Joyce Sidman. HMH Books for Young Readers (2010)

Hey You!: Poems to Skyscrapers, Mosquitoes, and Other Fun Things selected by Paul B. Janeczko. HarperCollins (2007)

Poetry Matters: Writing a Poem from the Inside Out by Ralph Fletcher. HarperCollins (2002)

Write a Poem Step by Step by JoAnn Early Macken. Earlybird Press (2012)

Websites

"April Rain Song" by Langston Hughes
www.poetryfoundation.org/features/video/6
Watch an animated video of the poem read by Langston Hughes.

"Tips for Poets: Observation" by Kristine O'Connell George:
www.kristinegeorge.com/tips_for_poets_observation.html
This informative website provides tips and guidance for young poets on using their own observations to inspire their own poetry.

National Poetry Month
www.poets.org/page.php/prmID/41
Celebrate National Poetry Month with the Academy of American Poets.

Poem in Your Pocket Day
www.poets.org/page.php/prmID/406
Learn all about Poem in Your Pocket Day!

Glossary

Note: Some boldfaced words are defined where they appear in the book.

alliteration A series of words that begin with the same sound

assonance A series of words with the same vowel sound

cluster A brainstorming technique that links related words together

consonance A series of words with the same consonant sound in the middles and/or at the ends

drama A story meant to be performed as a play

line break The end of a line in a poem

mask Writing a poem as though you were someone else

onomatopoeia Words that sound like they are spelled, sound effect words

point of view The speaker's position in relation to the story being told

prose The language we speak and write every day

rhyme Identical sounds at the ends of words

rhythm A pattern of regular sounds in a series of words

setting Time and place

stanza A group of lines in a poem

stressed Emphasized

thesaurus A book with lists of words that have similar meanings

voice The writer's tone or style

Index